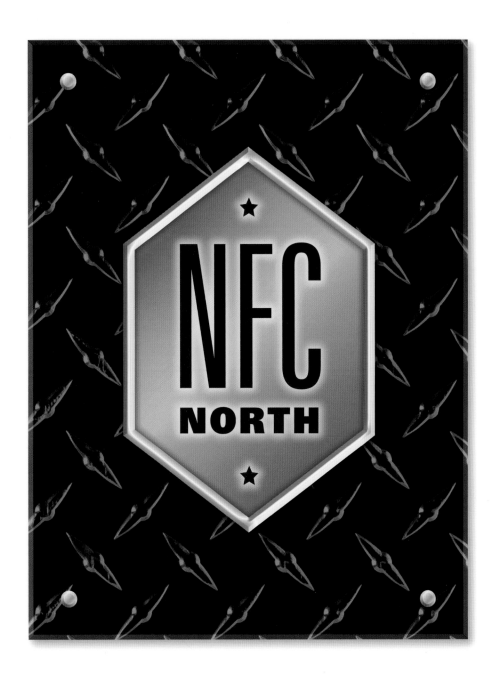

NFC NORTH

BY MICHAEL TEITELBAUM

★ Chicago Bears ★ Detroit Lions ★ Green Bay Packers ★ Minnesota Vikings ★

Published by The Child's World®
1980 Lookout Drive
Mankato, MN 56003-1705
800-599-READ
www.childsworld.com

The Child's World®: Mary Berendes, Publishing Director
The Design Lab: Kathleen Petelinsek, Design
Editorial Directions, Inc.: Pam Mamsch and E. Russell Primm,
Project Managers

Photographs ©: Robbins Photography (except page 25, AP)

Library of Congress Cataloging-in-Publication Data
Teitelbaum, Michael.
  NFC North / by Michael Teitelbaum.
    p. cm. Includes bibliographical references and index.
  ISBN 978-1-60973-132-8 (library reinforced : alk. paper)
  1. National Football League—History—Juvenile literature.
  2. Football—United States—History—Juvenile literature. I. Title.
  GV955.5.N35T45 2011
  796.332'640973—dc22   2011007402

Printed in the United States of America
Mankato, MN
May 2011
PA02093

TABLE OF
CONTENTS

4

First Season: 1920
NFL Championships: 9
Colors: Navy, Orange, and White
Mascot: Staley Da Bear

★

CHICAGO

BEARS

DA BEARS!

In 1920 eleven teams formed the American Professional
Football Association. One of those teams was the
Decatur Staleys, from Decatur, Illinois. George Halas
bought the Staleys and in 1921 moved them to Chicago.
The next year, he changed the team's name to the
Chicago Bears. That same year, the league changed its
name to the National Football League, and the
NFL was born.

Since then, "Da Bears," as their loyal fans in Chicago
call them, have won nine NFL championships, as well
as Super Bowl XX, after the 1985 season. The Bears
have more players (27) in the Pro Football Hall of Fame
than any other team. They have also won more NFL
games (more than 700) than any other pro team.

In 2008, running back Matt Forte ran for 1,238 yards to break the
Bears' team record for single-season rushing yards by a rookie.

HOME FIELD

The Bears have played at Soldier Field since 1971. In 2002, the team played at Memorial Stadium in Champaign, Illinois, while Soldier Field was gutted and rebuilt. The Bears returned to their rebuilt stadium the next year.

BIG DAYS

★ In 1963, before there was a Super Bowl, the Bears lost only one game. In the NFL championship game that year, the Bears beat the New York Giants 14–10 to capture the NFL's **crown**.

★ The Bears had their best season in 1985, winning 15 of their 16 games. In the playoffs, they **shut out** the New York Giants (21–0) and the Los Angeles Rams (24–0). Then, on January 26, 1986, the Bears crushed the New England Patriots (46–10) to win the Super Bowl.

★ The Bears returned to the Super Bowl following the 2006 season but lost to the Indianapolis Colts 29–17.

The Bears played their first game at Soldier Field against the Pittsburgh Steelers in 1971.

SUPERSTARS!

THEN

Dick Butkus, linebacker: one of the greatest defensive players
Walter Payton, running back: the NFL's second leading all-time rusher
Gale Sayers, running back: dominated the league for six years

NOW

Jay Cutler, quarterback: completes about 60 percent of his passes
Matt Forte, running back: the Bears' leading rusher
Johnny Knox, wide receiver: a Pro Bowler who leads the team in receptions
Brian Urlacher, linebacker: a four-time All-Pro who leads the team in tackles

★

STAT LEADERS

(All-time team leaders*)
Passing Yards: Sid Luckman, 14,686
Rushing Yards: Walter Payton, 16,726
Receiving Yards: Johnny Morris, 5,059
Touchdowns: Walter Payton, 125
Interceptions: Gary Fencik, 38

(*Through 2010 season.)

TIMELINE

1920
Bears, as the Decatur Staleys, are original member of what would become the NFL.

1921
Bears move to Chicago.

1922
Team name is changed to the Bears.

1932
Team wins its first championship as the Bears.

Linebacker Brian Urlacher has been selected to six Pro Bowl teams during his 11-year NFL career.

1940–1942
Bears win three NFL championships in a row.

1985
Bears win Super Bowl XX, beating the New England Patriots.

2006
Bears lose Super Bowl XLI to the Indianapolis Colts.

First Season: 1930
NFL Championships: 4
Colors: Blue and Silver
Mascot: Roary the Lion

★

DETROIT
LIONS

ROAR OF THE LION

In 1934 the Portsmouth (Ohio) Spartans of the NFL
moved to Detroit and became the Lions. In the
years since, the Detroit Lions have won four NFL
championships. The last time they won, however,
was in 1957.

The Lions are one of only four NFL teams that have
never been to the Super Bowl. In the 2008 season, they
became the only team in NFL history to lose all
16 games they played.

Although the team has not had much success
over the years, fans can look forward to one regular
tradition. Every year, the Lions play on Thanksgiving
Day in a game on national TV.

The Lions selected quarterback Matt Stafford as the
first overall pick in the 2009 NFL Draft.

HOME FIELD

The Lions have played in Ford Field since 2002. The stadium is unusual because it includes the former warehouse of Hudson's Department Stores. It also has the best sight lines in the league.

BIG DAYS

★ The Lions won their first NFL championship in 1935, beating the New York Giants 26–7.

★ In 1952 the Lions finished in a tie with the Los Angeles Rams and played a one-game **tiebreaker**. The Lions beat the Rams to qualify for the NFL championship game. Then they beat the Cleveland Browns 17–7 to claim their second NFL title.

★ The next year, the Lions won their second championship in a row, once again beating the Cleveland Browns, this time 17–16.

★ The Lions met the Browns again in 1957 for the NFL championship, which they won—pounding the Browns 59–14.

Ford Field can seat up to 65,000 Lions fans on game days.

SUPERSTARS!

THEN

Earl Clark, quarterback: the first great Lions star who led the team to its first NFL championship

Bobby Layne, quarterback: led the Lions through the 1950s, their most successful decade

Barry Sanders, running back: Hall of Famer who dominated the league from 1989 to 1998

★

NOW

Jahvid Best, running back: leads the team in rushing

Louis Delmas, defensive back: leads the team in tackles

Shaun Hill, quarterback: has completed more than 60 percent of his passes

Calvin Johnson, wide receiver: leads the Lions in receiving yardage

STAT LEADERS

(All-time team leaders*)

Passing Yards: Bobby Layne, 15,710

Rushing Yards: Barry Sanders, 15,269

Receiving Yards: Herman Moore, 9,174

Touchdowns: Barry Sanders, 109

Interceptions: Dick LeBeau, 62

(*Through 2010 season.)

TIMELINE

1934
Portsmouth Spartans move to Detroit and become the Detroit Lions.

1935
Lions win their first NFL championship.

1952 AND 1953
Lions win back-to-back NFL championships, led by Hall of Fame quarterback Bobby Layne.

Receiver Calvin Johnson has had 13 100-yard games in his four-year NFL career.

1991

Lions host their first home playoff game since 1957.

2008

Lions become the first NFL team to lose all 16 games they play.

16

First Season: 1919
NFL Championships: 13
Colors: Green, Gold,
and White
Mascot: None

★

GREEN BAY
PACKERS

"WINNING ISN'T EVERYTHING . . . IT'S THE ONLY THING!"

Earl "Curly" Lambeau organized the Green Bay Packers in 1919. Two years later, the Packers joined the brand-new National Football League. Little did Lambeau realize that the Packers would go on to be the most successful team in the history of the NFL.

The Green Bay Packers have won the most NFL championships of any NFL team. They won the first two Super Bowls ever played, in 1967 and 1968, a third Super Bowl in 1996, and a fourth in 2010! Vince Lombardi, their legendary coach from 1959 to 1967, turned a losing team around and led them to five NFL titles in a seven-year period. His philosophy? "Winning isn't everything . . . it's the only thing!"

Six-time Pro Bowl cornerback Charles Woodson was named NFL Defensive Player of the Year in 2009.

HOME FIELD

The Packers have played in eight different stadiums. They've been in their current stadium, Lambeau Field, since 1957. It's named for Curly Lambeau, the man who started the team in 1919.

BIG DAYS

★ In 1929, the Packers went **undefeated** and won the first of their record-setting 13 NFL championships.

★ In 1959, after a miserable 1–10–1 finish the year before, the Packers hired Vince Lombardi. He immediately led them to a 7–5 record.

★ Following another championship in the 1966 season, the Packers won the first Super Bowl, beating Kansas City 35–10.

★ Battling –13 degrees Fahrenheit (–25 degrees Celsius) temperatures and –46°F (–43°C) windchills, the Packers won the "Ice Bowl" in 1967 when quarterback Bart Starr dove into the end zone from one yard out. That gave the Packers a 21–17 win over the Dallas Cowboys. It was their third straight NFL championship and sent them to their second straight Super Bowl.

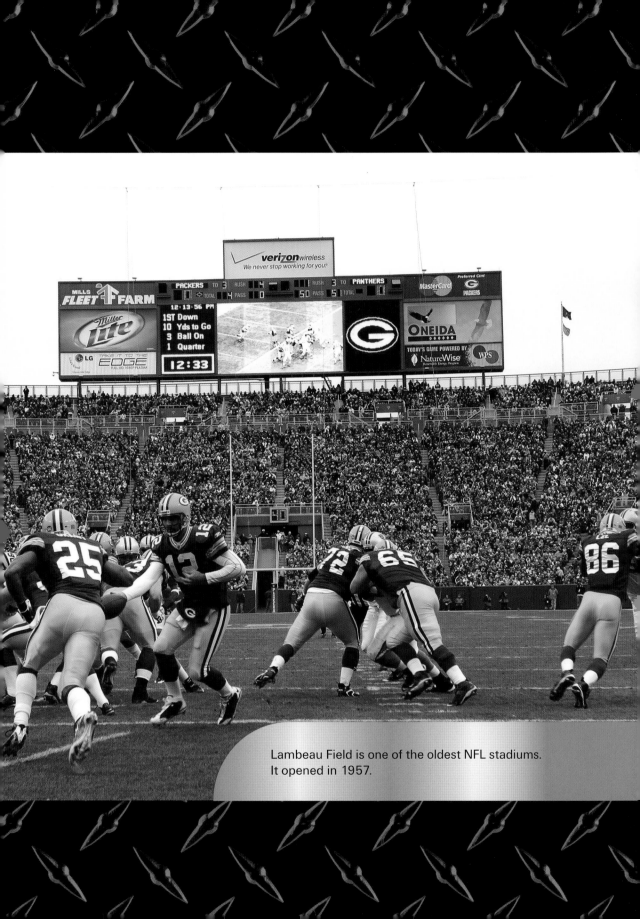

Lambeau Field is one of the oldest NFL stadiums. It opened in 1957.

SUPERSTARS!

THEN

Brett Favre, quarterback: three-time league MVP, led the Packers back to Super Bowl glory

Vince Lombardi, coach: rescued a failing **franchise** and led the team to NFL dominance

Ray Nitschke, linebacker: one of the best linebackers in NFL history

Bart Starr, quarterback: led the team to five NFL championships and two Super Bowls

NOW

Donald Driver, wide receiver: one of the top receivers in the league

Aaron Rodgers, quarterback: took over for Brett Favre in 2010 and is becoming one of the best quarterbacks in the league

Charles Woodson, cornerback: one of the NFL's top defensive players

STAT LEADERS

(All-time team leaders*)

Passing Yards: Brett Favre, 61,655

Rushing Yards: Ahman Green, 8,322

Receiving Yards: James Lofton, 9,656

Touchdowns: Don Hutson, 105

Interceptions: Bobby Dillon, 52

(*Through 2010 season.)

TIMELINE

1919
Green Bay Packers formed by Curly Lambeau.

1921
Packers join the NFL.

1929
Packers win their first NFL championship.

1959
Coach Vince Lombardi arrives to turn around the failing team.

Aaron Rodgers was the first quarterback in NFL history to rack up more than 4,000 passing yards in both of his first two seasons as a starter.

1967 AND 1968

Packers win Super Bowls I and II.

1996

Packers win Super Bowl XXXI.

2010

Packers win Super Bowl XLV.

First Season: 1961
NFL Championships: 0
Colors: Purple, Gold, and White
Mascot: Ragnar the Viking

★

VIKINGS

THE PURPLE PEOPLE EATERS

In 1961, the NFL **expanded**, and the Minnesota Vikings were born. In the years since, they have been one of the most successful teams in the NFL, although they have never won a championship.

The Vikings have been to four Super Bowls but lost each time. They have the second-most playoff appearances (26) in the league, and the most AFC or NFC championship game appearances (9) without winning a Super Bowl.

In the 1970s, their defense was nicknamed the Purple People Eaters for the way they "gobbled up" running backs and receivers. One member of that defense, Alan Page, was voted the NFL's Most Valuable Player in 1971. Page became the first defensive player to ever win the award.

Twenty-year veteran quarterback Brett Favre retired after the 2010 season.

HOME FIELD

When the Vikings started in 1961, they played at Metropolitan Stadium. Since 1982 the Hubert H. Humphrey Metrodome has been their home.

BIG DAYS

★ In 1969, the Vikings had the best record in the league (12–2). They became the first expansion team to reach the Super Bowl. Although they were heavily favored to win, they lost the Super Bowl to the AFL's Kansas City Chiefs 23–7.

★ In 1973, the Vikings again posted a 12–2 record and made it to the Super Bowl. They lost to the Miami Dolphins 21–7.

★ After the 1974 season, the Vikings appeared in their second straight Super Bowl, this time losing to the Pittsburgh Steelers 16–6.

★ Two years later, the Vikings made it to the Super Bowl for the fourth time, but once again lost. The Oakland Raiders beat them 32–14.

The 64,111-seat Mall of America Field at
Hubert H. Humphrey Metrodome opened in 1982.

SUPERSTARS!

THEN

Carl Eller, defensive end: feared member of the "Purple People Eaters"

Bud Grant, coach: Hall of Fame coach who led the Vikings during their most successful years

Alan Page, defensive tackle: first defensive player to win the NFL's MVP Award

Fran Tarkenton, quarterback: one of the dominant quarterbacks in the NFL in the 1960s and '70s

NOW

Percy Harvin, wide receiver: favorite passing target

Adrian Peterson, running back: one of the top running backs in the league

Visanthe Shiancoe, tight end: leads the team in yards per reception

STAT LEADERS

(All-time team leaders*)

Passing Yards: Fran Tarkenton, 33,098

Rushing Yards: Robert Smith, 6,818

Receiving Yards: Cris Carter, 12,383

Touchdowns: Cris Carter, 110

Interceptions: Paul Krause, 53

★

TIMELINE

(*Through 2010 season.)

1961
Minnesota Vikings form as part of NFL expansion.

1967
Vikings hire Bud Grant, who becomes the winningest coach in their history.

1969
Vikings play in their first Super Bowl.

1972
Vikings reacquire quarterback Fran Tarkenton, who started his career in Minnesota.

As a rookie, running back Adrian Peterson was the MVP of the 2007 Pro Bowl.

1973 AND 1974

The team plays in back-to-back Super Bowls.

1976

Vikings lose their fourth Super Bowl, bringing their record to 0-4 in the big game.

2007

Vikings draft running back Adrian Peterson, who goes on to dominate the league.

STAT
STUFF

NFC NORTH DIVISION STATISTICS*

Team	All-Time Record (W-L-T)	NFL Titles (Most Recent)	Times in NFL Playoffs
Chicago Bears	704–512–42	9 (1985)	25
Detroit Lions	496–593–32	4 (1957)	14
Green Bay Packers	664–524–36	13 (2010)	25
Minnesota Vikings	413–336–9	0	26

NFC NORTH DIVISION CHAMPIONSHIPS
(MOST RECENT)

Chicago Bears . . . 22 (2010)

Detroit Lions . . . 8 (1993)

Green Bay Packers . . . 19 (2004)

Minnesota Vikings . . . 18 (2009)

(*Through 2010 season.)

Position Key:
QB: Quarterback
RB: Running back
WR: Wide receiver
C: Center
T: Tackle
G: Guard
CB: Cornerback
LB: Linebacker
DE: Defensive end
PK: Place kicker
TE: Tight end

NFC NORTH PRO FOOTBALL
HALL OF FAME MEMBERS

Chicago Bears
Doug Atkins, WR
George Blanda,
  QB, PK
Dick Butkus, LB
Guy Chambers, DE
George Connor, T
Jimmy Conzelman,
  RB
Richard Dent, DE
Mike Ditka, TE
Paddy Driscoll, RB
Jim Finks, General
  Manager
Danny Fortmann, G
Bill George, G, LB
Red Grange, RB
George Halas,
  Coach
Dan Hampton, DE
Ed Healey, T
Bill Hewitt, DE
Stan Jones, T
Walt Kiesling, G
Bobby Layne, QB
Sid Luckman, QB
Link Lyman, T
George McAfee,
  RB
George Musso, G

Bronko Nagurski,
  RB
Alan Page, T
Walter Payton, RB
Gale Sayers, RB
Mike Singletary, LB
Joe Stydahar, T
George Trafton, C
Bulldog Turner, C

Detroit Lions
Lem Barney, CB
Jack Christiansen,
  RB
Earl Clark, QB
Lou Creekmur, T
Bill Dudley, RB
Frank Gatski, C
John Henry
  Johnson, RB
Dick Lane, CB
Yale Lary, CB
Bobby Layne, QB
Dick LeBeau, CB
Ollie Matson, RB
Hugh McElhenny,
  RB
Barry Sanders, RB
Charlie Sanders, TE
Joe Schmidt, LB

Doak Walker, RB

**Green Bay
Packers**
Alex
  Wojciechowicz, C
Herb Adderley, CB
Tony Canadeo, RB
Willie Davis, DE
Len Ford, DE
Forrest Gregg, T
Ted Hendricks, LB
Arnie Herber, QB
Clarke Hinkle, RB
Paul Hornung, RB
Cal Hubbard, T
Don Hutson, WR
Henry Jordan, T
Walt Kiesling, G
Curly Lambeau,
  Coach
James Lofton, WR
Vince Lombardi,
  Coach
John McNally, RB
Mike Michalske, G
Ray Nitschke, LB
Jim Ringo, C
Bart Starr, QB
Jan Stenerud, PK

Jim Taylor, RB
Emlen Tunnell, CB
Reggie White, DE
Willie Wood, CB

**Minnesota
Vikings**
Dave Casper, TE
Carl Eller, DE
Jim Finks, General
  Manager
Bud Grant, Coach
Paul Krause, CB
Jim Langer, C
Randall McDaniel,
  G
Hugh McElhenny,
  RB
Warren Moon, QB
Alan Page, T
John Randle, T
Jan Stenerud, PK
Fran Tarkenton, QB
Ron Yary, T
Gary Zimmerman, T

NOTE: Includes players
with at least three
seasons with the team.
Players may appear with
more than one team.

GLOSSARY

★

crown (KROUN): championship

dominated (DAH-muh-na-ted): completely controlled; the best by far

expanded (ek-SPAN-did): added new teams to the league

franchise (FRAN-chize): the right or license of a team to call itself a certain name

shut out (SHUHT OUT): to stop the opposing team from scoring

tiebreaker (TYE-bray-kur): a game played when two teams end the regular season with the same record, to determine who goes to the playoffs

tradition (truh-DISH-uhn): an event that occurs regularly

undefeated (uhn-di-FEET-did): winning every game a team plays

FIND OUT MORE

★

BOOKS

Buckley, James, Jr. *Scholastic Ultimate Guide to Football*.
New York: Franklin Watts, 2009.

MacRae, Sloan. *The Chicago Bears*. New York:
PowerKids Press, 2011.

MacRae, Sloan. *The Green Bay Packers*. New York:
PowerKids Press, 2011.

Stewart, Mark. *The Detroit Lions*. Chicago: Norwood
House Press, 2010.

Stewart, Mark. *The Minnesota Vikings*. Chicago:
Norwood House Press, 2009.

★

WEB SITES

For links to learn more about football visit
www.childsworld.com/links

INDEX

32

ABOUT THE AUTHOR

Michael Teitelbaum has been a writer and editor of children's books and magazines for more than 20 years. He was editor of *Little League Magazine* and *Spider-Man Magazine* for Marvel Comics. He is the author of a two-volume encyclopedia on the Baseball Hall of Fame. Teitelbaum and his wife, Sheleigh, live in a 170-year-old farmhouse in the Catskill Mountains of upstate New York.